Kobe Bryant

The Black Mamba Inspirational Life From Kid To Legend

©Copyright 2020

By LA SPORT

All rights reserved. This document is geared towards providing exact and reliable information with regards to the topic and issue covered. The publication is sold with the idea that the publisher is not required to render accounting, officially permitted, or otherwise, qualified services. If advice is necessary, legal or professional, a practiced individual in the profession should be ordered. -From a Declaration of Principles which was accepted and approved equally by a Committee of the American Bar Association and a Committee of Publishers and Associations. In no way is it legal to reproduce, duplicate, or transmit any part of this document in either electronic means or in printed format. Recording of this publication is strictly prohibited and any storage of this document is not allowed unless with written permission from the publisher. All rights reserved. The information provided herein is stated to be truthful and consistent, in that any liability, in terms of inattention or otherwise, by any usage or abuse of any policies, processes, or directions contained within is the solitary and utter responsibility of the recipient reader. Under no circumstances will any legal responsibility or blame be held against the publisher for any reparation, damages, or monetary loss due to the information herein, either directly or indirectly. Respective authors own all copyrights not held by the publisher. The information herein is offered for informational purposes solely, and is universal as so. The presentation of the information is without contract or any type of guarantee assurance. The trademarks that are used are without any consent, and the publication of the trademark is without permission or backing by the trademark owner. All trademarks and brands within this book are for clarifying purposes only and are the owned by the owners themselves, not affiliated with this document.

Introduction

Kobe Bryant was an American well-known basketball player. A capturing protect, Bryant entered the national Basketball affiliation (NBA) directly from high school and played his entire 20-season professional career inside the league with the Los Angeles Lakers. Bryant won five NBA championships, changed into an 18-time All-superstar, 15-time member of the All-NBA crew; a 12-time member of the All-protective team turned into named the 2008 NBA most precious participant (MVP) and changed into a -time NBA Finals MVP winner. One of the greatest players regarded as of all time, he led the NBA in scoring at some stage in two seasons, ranks 4th at the league's all-time regular-season scoring and all-time postseason scoring lists.

He attended Lower Merion excessive school in Pennsylvania, wherein he changed into identified as the pinnacle excessive-college basketball player in the USA. Upon commencement, he declared for the 1996 NBA draft and changed into decided on with the aid of the Charlotte Hornets with the thirteenth universal choice; the Hornets then traded him to the Lakers. As a rookie, Bryant earned himself recognition as an excessive-flyer and a fan preferred by prevailing the 1997 Slam Dunk Contest, and he became named an All-megastar by using his 2nd season. Despite a feud with teammate Shaquille O'Neal, the pair led the Lakers to 3 consecutive NBA championships from 2000 to 2002. In 2003, Bryant was accused of sexual assault. Criminal costs had been delivered after which dropped after the accuser refused to testify, with a civil in shape later settled out of court. Bryant denied the attack price, however, admitted to a sexual come across, and issued a public apology; however, the allegations had been considered to have harmed his public profile and caused the loss of numerous sponsorships.

When Lakers Lost the 2004 NBA Championships, O'Neal changed into traded, and Bryant became the keystone of the Lakers. He commanded the NBA in scoring during the 2005–06 and 2006–07 seasons. In 2006, he scored a profession-high 81 points; the second-most points scored in a single sport in league records, in the back of Wilt Chamberlain's 100-point game in 1962. Bryant led the team to 2 consecutive championships in 2009 and 2010 and was named NBA Finals MVP on both occasions. He persevered to be the various pinnacle gamers in the league via 2013, while he suffered a torn Achilles tendon at age 34. Although he recovered from that damage, he suffered season-ending accidents to his knee and shoulder, respectively, in the following seasons.

Mentioning his bodily decline, Bryant retired after the 2015–16 season.

At 34 years and 104 days of age, Bryant has become the youngest participant in league history to reach 30,000 career factors. He became the best-ever leading scorer in Lakers franchise history on February 1, 2010, surpassing Jerry West. Bryant turned into also the primary protect in NBA history to play at the least 20 seasons. His 18 All-superstar designations are the second-most all-time, at the same time as it's far the document for most consecutive appearances as a starter. Bryant's four All-famous person MVP Awards are tied with Bob Pettit for the most in NBA history. At the 2008 and 2012 summer season Olympics, he received two gold medals as a member of the U.S. National group. In 2018, he received the

Academy Award for quality lively brief film for his 2017 movie expensive Basketball.

Former pro basketball participant Kobe Bryant gained 5 NBA titles with the Los Angeles Lakers even as establishing himself as one in every of the sport's all-time greats.

"I heard the ball bouncing. No lights were on. Practice was at about 11, it was probably about 9, 9:30. And I go out to the court and I look, and there's Kobe Bryant. He's out there shooting in the dark. And I stood there for probably about ten seconds, and I said, 'This kid is gonna be great.' Byron Scott

Kobe Bryant inspired a generation of basketball players worldwide with sublime skills and an unquenchable competitive fire.

He earned Los Angeles' eternal adoration during his two decades as the fierce soul of the beloved Lakers, and he was respected by basketball fans from every place with a hoop and a dream, including his native Philadelphia and in Italy, his other childhood home.

Less than four years into his retirement, Bryant was seizing new challenges and working to inspire his daughters' generation through sports and storytelling when his next chapter ended shockingly early.

Bryant established a reputation for taking shots in the closing moments of tight games, even when he was double or triple-teamed, and was noted as one of the premier closers in the NBA. In a 2012 annual survey of NBA general managers, Bryant was selected for the 10th consecutive season as the player general managers would want to take a clutch shot with a game on the line. Bryant enjoyed being the villain, and reveled in being booed and then silencing the crowd with his play.

His ability to make difficult shots has also drawn criticism of his shot selection. Throughout his career, Bryant was disparaged for being a selfish, high-volume shooter; he missed more field goal attempts in his career than any other player in NBA history. [g] Phil Jackson, who coached Bryant for many years, stated that Bryant "tends to force the action, especially when the game isn't going his way. When his shot is off, Kobe will pound away relentlessly until his luck turns."

According to Bryant, "I would go 0 for 30 before I would go 0 for 9; 0 for 9 means you beat yourself, you psyched yourself out of the game."

In addition to his abilities on offense, Bryant also established himself as a standout defensive player. Bryant rarely drew charges when he played defense, which he believed spared his body and contributed to his longevity. Some critics have suggested that Bryant's defensive accolades in his later years were based more on his reputation than his actual play

Bryant was also lauded for his work ethic. Throughout his first 16 seasons, his body was resilient, and he exhibited a high pain threshold while often playing through injuries. A fierce competitor, Bryant made opponents and teammates alike the objects of his scorn. Many players have considered him difficult to play with because of his high level of commitment and performance.

According to sportswriter Mark Heisler of Forbes, "Kobe was the most alienated superstar the NBA had ever seen." He did, however, lead the Lakers to two championships after the departure of Shaquille O'Neal; during this period, he became more of a mentor to his teammates than he had been earlier in his careerBryant's longtime head coach Phil Jackson noted that the biggest difference between his first and second stints in coaching the Lakers was if Bryant talked to teammates in his earlier years with the Lakers, it was usually, "Give me the damn ball." During the latter period, "[Bryant] embraced the team and his teammates, calling them up when we were on the road and inviting them out to dinner. It was as if the other players were now his partners, not his personal spear-carriers"

Who Was Kobe Bryant?

Kobe Bryant spent his early years in Italy and joined the NBA instantly out of excessive faculty. A dominant scorer, Bryant won five NBA championships and the 2008 MVP Award with the la Lakers. Even though later seasons had been marred through accidents, he exceeded

Michael Jordan for third place at the NBA all-time scoring listing in December 2014 and retired in 2016 after scoring 60 factors in his final game. In 2018, Bryant earned an Academy Award for the first-rate animated quick movie for Dear Basketball. On January 26, 2020, he turned into a helicopter crash that killed Bryant, his thirteen-yr-antique daughter Gigi and seven others.

Bryant died at age forty-one alongside his 13-year-old daughter Gianna and seven others in a helicopter crash in Calabasas, California.

Table Of Content

CHAPTER 1 18

Kobe Bryant 18

    Gianna visible as inheritor to an unrivaled legacy 30

    James and Bryant have a final conversation 33

    Bryant used helicopters like most take Ubers 35

    The pilot climbed better to keep away from a cloud layer 37

    Fans are barred access to a disaster website online 40

CHAPTER 2 43

Kobe Bryant Professional career 43

    Adolescence 49

    NBA career and Stats 51

    Retirement 53

    Academy Award for 'pricey Basketball.' 56

    Sexual assault fee 58

    Philanthropy 58

    Kobe Bryant's circle of relatives 59

    Wife and kids 59

Childhood 60

    High college 61

    Adjusting to the NBA 62

- Three-peat 63
- Championships 64

Career ranking 65
- Career – season 65
- Career – playoffs 66
- NBA awards and accomplishments 67

NBA records 70
- Currently holds 70
- Kobe Bryant's legendary NBA career summed up in 8 eye-popping stats 74
- Kobe Bryant's Stats, Highlights, and Reaction from Final NBA Game ... 79

CHAPTER 3 83

Kobe Bryant's most inspirational quotes 83
- Kobe Bryant on achieving achievement: 84
- His recommendation to Gordon Hayward about returning rehabbing damage: 84
- At the mission of coming back from accidents: 85
- Ongoing straight from high school to the NBA: 86
- On figuring out, he changed into specific from other NBA gamers: 86
- On failure: 87
- On no longer being scared of failure: 87
- On making sacrifices: 88
- On what it takes to steer: 89
- On prevailing his first championship: 90

On retiring and facing the stop of his basketball career: 90

CHAPTER 4 92

The Kobe Bryant Guide to Life: Inspirational Tips to Become More Successful 92

Final phrases 101

Kobe Bryant: His most inspiring quotes on life and basketball 101

On accomplishing a tranquil thoughts 110

On perseverance 112

On the impossibility of perfection 112

On preparing for surgical operation 113

On making sacrifices for a dream 113

On failure 114

More than a number: College players tell their stories about Kobe Bryant inspiring them to wear No. 24 114

Sacred heart junior E.J. Anosike (East Orange, New Jersey) 116

Creighton junior Mitch Ballock (Eudora, Kansas) 120

How Kobe Bryant is Inspiring the Next Generation 128

Chapter1

Kobe Bryant

Bryant was born in Philadelphia, the youngest of three youngsters and most effective son of former NBA player Joe Bryant and Pamela Cox Bryant. He became the maternal nephew of basketball player John "overweight" Cox additionally. His mother and father named him after the famous beef of Kobe, Japan, which they saw on an eating place menu. His center name, Bean, become derived from his father's nickname "Jellybean." Bryant's family become Catholic, and he had usually practiced his religion.

Bryant started playing basketball while he changed into elderly 3, and the Lakers were his preferred group while he turned into developing up. While Bryant became six, his father retired from the NBA and moved his family to Rieti in Italy to retain playing expert basketball at a lower degree. After years, they moved first to Reggio Calabria, then to Pistoia and Reggio Emilia. Kobe became familiar with his new way of life and found out to speak fluent Italian. He became explicitly keen on Reggio Emilia, which he was taken into consideration a loving region and wherein some of his first-rate childhood reminiscences have been made. Bryant commenced playing basketball significantly at the same time as living in Reggio Emilia. Bryant's grandfather could mail him videos of NBA video games for Bryant to take a look at. He also discovered to play football, and his preferred football team became A.C. Milan. For summers, Bryant could come again to the USA to play in a basketball summer season league. While Bryant changed into 13, he and his own family moved returned to Philadelphia.

Bryant earned national recognition at some point in a remarkable high school profession at decrease Merion excessive college in Ardmore, positioned within the Philadelphia suburb of Lower Merion. He played on the varsity basketball group as a freshman. Bryant has become the primary freshman in a long time to start to decrease Merion's varsity group; however, the crew completed with a 4–20 document. In the subsequent three years, the Aces compiled a seventy-seven–thirteen file, with Bryant playing all five positions. Throughout his junior yr, he averaged 31.1 factors, 10.4 rebounds, and five.2 assists and changed into named Pennsylvania player of the year while additionally incomes a fourth-crew Parade All-American nomination, attracting attention from university recruiters within the method. Duke, Michigan, North Carolina, and Villanova were on the top of his list. But, after high schooler Kevin Garnett went inside the first spherical of the 1995 NBA draft, Bryant also began taking into consideration going immediately to the professionals.

At Adidas ABCD camp, Bryant earned the 1995 senior MVP award at the same time as playing along future NBA teammate Lamar Odom. At the same time, as in excessive college, then 76ers educate John Lucas invited Bryant to work out and scrimmage with the team, wherein he played one-on-one with Jerry Stackhouse. In his senior year of high faculty, Bryant led the Aces to their first national championship in 53 years. During the run, he averaged 30. Eight factors, 12 rebounds, 6. Five assists, four steals, and 3.8 blocked pictures in leading the Aces to a 31–three document. Bryant ended his excessive faculty profession as Southeastern Pennsylvania's all-time leading scorer at 2,883 points, surpassing both Wilt Chamberlain and Lionel Simmons.

Bryant received several awards for his excellent performance all through his senior 12 months at decrease Merion. Those blanketed being named Naismith high school participant of the year, Gatorade men's countrywide Basketball player of the year, a McDonald's All-American, a first-team Parade All-American and an America today All-USA first crew participant. Bryant's varsity educates, Greg Downer, commented that he became "a complete participant who dominates" and praised his work ethic, even as the crew's top participant. In 1996, Bryant took R&B singer Brandy to his senior prom. In the end, the 17-12 months-antique Bryant made the selection to move without delay into the NBA, turning into best the 6th participant in NBA history to do so. Bryant's information turned into met with a whole lot of publicity at a time, while prep-to-seasoned NBA gamers had been no longer very common (Garnett being the only exception in two decades). His basketball skills and SAT score of 1080 could have ensured admission to any university he chose, but he did not officially visit any campuses. In 2012, Bryant became revered as one of the 35 best McDonald's All-Americans.

Bryant's father, Joe ("Jelly Bean") Bryant, become a professional basketball player who spent eight seasons in the NBA and eight greater playings in Italy, in which Bryant went to school. While his family lowers back to us, Bryant played basketball at lower Merion excessive college in Ardmore, Pennsylvania, in which he acquired numerous countrywide players of the year rewards and ruined the southeastern Pennsylvania recording document set using Wilt Chamberlain with 2,883 factors. Bryant opted to forgo college and declared him eligible for the NBA draft while he graduated from high college. The Charlotte Hornets selected him with the thirteenth selection of the 1996 draft. He changed into traded to the Lakers shortly after that and has become the second one youngest NBA player in records while the 1996–ninety-seven seasons opened. He fast proved his merit with the Lakers and changed into decided on for the NBA All-star recreation in only his 2nd season, becoming the youngest All-celebrity.

Bryant became pressured to proportion the function of the Lakers' celebrity player with his famous and talented teammate Shaquille O'Neal. The 2 had an uneasy dating, but they found achievement underneath the leadership of Phil Jackson, who became train of the Lakers in 1999. Bryant, a shooting protect, and O'Neal, a center, meshed right into a remarkably effective aggregate, and, by the point, Bryant turned into 23, the Lakers had received three consecutive NBA championships.

Inside the 2003 playoffs, the Lakers have been defeated in the second spherical. Several months later, Bryant turned into accused of raping a younger lady in Colorado. He maintained his innocence, and all expenses have been ultimately dropped. At the same time, the woman refused to testify after a month's long campaign of harassment through enthusiasts of Bryant and some members of the media. (Bryant later apologized, admitting that he found out his accuser did now not accept as accurate with their sexual encounter become consensual, and a local match was settled in 2005.) The incident greatly tarnished his picture. Led via Bryant, the Lakers again to the finals in 2004, however, they were upset through the Detroit Pistons. O'Neal sooner or later turned into traded, and Bryant emerged as the crew's sole leader.

Bryant led the league in scoring throughout the 2005–06 and 2006–07 seasons, and in 2008 he become named the league's MVP for the first time in his career. Bryant received his fourth NBA name in 2009, and he was named the finals MVP after averaging a stellar 32.4 points per game within the series. He led the Lakers to their 0.33 immediately Western convention championship in 2009–10, and he turned into over again named NBA finals MVP after the Lakers defeated the Boston Celtics in a seven-game series. The Lakers won division titles in each of the subsequent seasons however were removed in the 2nd round of each postseason. Coming into the 2012–thirteen season, the Lakers introduced superstars Steve Nash and Dwight Howard to their lineup and have been taken into consideration one of the preseason name favorites. However, the disappointing group becomes slightly on pace to qualify for the final Western convention playoff spot. At the same time, Bryant ruptured his Achilles tendon in April 2013, inflicting him to miss the rest of the season. (The Lakers have been in the end the 8th and final playoff seed that season and have been swept in their first collection.) He returned to the court in December 2013 but played in only six games earlier than fracturing his kneecap and lacking the remainder of that season as nicely. Bryant lowers back for the beginning of the 2014–15 seasons before he changed into once more injured, tearing his rotator cuff in January

2015. He played almost all of the following season however again struggled, with a profession-low .358 capturing percentage even as averaging 17.6 points per sport, and he retired following the remaining ordinary-season game of the 2015–sixteen season.

Further to his professional accomplishments, he was a member of the gold medal-prevailing U.S. Guys's basketball groups at the 2008 Beijing Olympic video games and the 2012 London Olympic video games. In 2015 Bryant wrote the poem "Dear Basketball," and two years later, it served as the premise for a short movie of the same call, which he additionally narrated. The paintings gained an Academy Award for the quality animated quick film. In 2018 Bryant posted the ebook The Mamba Mentality: How I Play, in which he defined his approach to basketball; the identity reflected a nickname he bestowed upon himself in the course of his gambling days, "The Black Mamba." On January 26, 2020, Bryant and his thirteen-12 months-antique daughter had been amongst a group journeying to a girls basketball sport in a helicopter when it crashed, killing all nine human beings aboard.

Droplets of holy water shone at the brow of one of the most recognizable faces in sports as he made his way through the chapel earlier than the early Mass last Sunday on the parish in Newport seaside, California.

Kobe Bryant, 41, an 18-time All celebrity who gained 5 NBA championships with the la Lakers, shook fingers with Father Steve Sallot and requested approximately making his confirmation, a sacrament that could solidify his commitment to the Catholic Church.

It would have been hard to now not note one of the greatest basketball players of all time. But Bryant had tried continuously to skip as just every other one of the trustworthy, regularly sitting in a rear pew, so he failed to distract from the solemn priority at hand.

That unforgettable day began with Bryant stopping for a moment of prayer and mirrored image. It would lead to a violent overwhelm of metallic and flames.

Bryant, his 13-12 months-old daughter, Gianna, and seven others perished Sunday, January 26, inside the remote hills of Calabasas. The excessive-velocity impact unleashed surprise waves across the globe.

Gianna visible as inheritor to an unrivaled legacy

After a glittering, straight-out-of-high-faculty 20-year NBA profession, Bryant becomes regularly seen with Gianna -- a skilled younger participant -- at basketball games. Convinced she too was sure for glory, he saw the second one of his four daughters -- alongside Natalia, Bianka, and Capri -- with spouse Vanessa Laine Bryant as heir to his greatness.

Closing Sunday, Bryant changed into to instruct Gianna's woman Mambas team in opposition to the Fresno girl warmness at his Mamba sports Academy within the northern la suburb of thousand very well. The Mamba Cup tournament had already all started, providing boys' and girls' groups from 0.33 via eighth grades.

Gianna had her father's competitive streak. An aspiring WNBA player, she often took a problem with strangers' hints that her dad and mom needed a son to uphold the Bryant legacy.

"She's like, 'Oy, I was given this,'" Bryant said for the duration of a 2018 appearance on ABC's "Jimmy Kimmel stays!" "I am like, this is right. Sure, you do, you purchased this."

The day earlier than the Fresno game, a basketball- and Kobe-obsessed 13-year-vintage named Brady Smigiel had performed within the Mamba Cup along with his twin brother, Beau. Past the courtroom, the youngster had committed -- in some unspecified time in the future throughout event play -- to securing a selfie with his idol.

But Gianna's travel crew had misplaced its first Saturday recreation, 46-29. And Bryant's signature hate-to-lose mentality became glaring.

"Kobe becomes mad they lost," Brady told his mom.

The NBA legend wouldn't mug for Brady's digicam. But he raised his hand, balled up a fist and bumped knuckles -- a younger player's dream come authentic.

The woman Mambas received their 2nd game that day. Later on, their train milled round off courtroom. Brady got near. He flashed a broad grin, positioned his lens, and -- click on -- managed a blurry selfie with a towering Bryant within the historical past.

All megastar-turned-prep teach once more failed to forestall, Smigiel recalled. But he knew what Brady without a doubt desired.

Bryant addressed her son: "we're going to get a higher p.C day after today."

James and Bryant have a final conversation

Hours later, Bryant was on Twitter, congratulating Laker's celeb LeBron James for passing him as the 1/3 maximum scorer in NBA history with 33,655 factors. Bryant had scored 33,643 points in his brilliant pro profession.

"Continuing to move the game forward, @KingJames," he tweeted. "plenty respect my brother."

It turned into in Philadelphia, where Bryant was born on August 23, 1978, that James has become the game's third maximum scorer.

On Instagram, Bryant posted a photo with James: "directly to #2. Maintain developing the game and charting the path for the following."

But social media couldn't comprise their adoration. These men -- pillars of their profession, cultural touchstones, with names already inked into records -- had to talk.

"I just heard your voice Sunday morning before I left Philly to go again to l. A.," LeBron wrote afterward Instagram, relating to a congratulatory call from Bryant. "Failed to assume for one bit in a million years that might be the ultimate communication we might have."

Bryant used helicopters like most take Ubers

No longer long after stepping out of our woman Queen of Angels, Bryant waited to board a chartered helicopter at John Wayne Airport in Orange County. He took made the flight to a thousand.

Gianna was there, at the side of her teammates: Alyssa Altobelli and Payton Chester.

Also on deck to take off were Alyssa's parents, John and Keri; Payton's mother, Sarah; assistant ladies basketball coach Christina Mauser; and helicopter pilot Ara Zobayan.

It changed into a much less-than-ideal day to fly in Southern California. Visibility turned into so low la' police pressure grounded its choppers.

Nonetheless, in sprawling and visitors-choked Los Angeles, celebrities depend on helicopters the way the majority take Ubers.

In his playing days, Bryant has been recognized to take a personal helicopter from his Orange County home to each home game in la' Staples center. It gave the capturing shield a more excellent time with his kids. It helped preserve his battered knees, returned, and feet in the course of the long season.

Ready Sunday morning on the tarmac for the woman Mambas group became a Sikorsky S-76B, a workhorse with an impeccable safety file. It became a version Bryant favored.

"It's the flying Lincoln town car for executives," aviation analyst Miles O'Brien stated.

The helicopter Bryant deliberate to board becomes owned using Island explicit maintaining Corp of Van Nuys. Past charters, it marketed flights to Catalina Island, aerial tours and excursion packages.

Federal policies did not require the aircraft to have a terrain consciousness and warning gadget, a protection characteristic those indicators pilots when they may hit land. It also didn't have to convey a cockpit voice recorder and a flight data recorder that could notably aid investigators in case of disaster.

The pilot climbed better to keep away from a cloud layer

With Bryant and the others nestled on board, the aircraft took off at 9:06 a.m. PT.

"Helicopter 2EX, preserve outdoor Burbank elegance C airspace. I've an aircraft going around," an air visitor's controller radioed the pilot about 15 mins later, in step with recorded excerpts.

The copter circled over Glendale, close to the town of Burbank.

"2EX, protecting," spoke back Zobayan, a device-certified pilot who earned his business pilot's license in 2007.

Zobayan turned into skilled. He'd had eight, two hundred hours of flight time as of July. At the S-seventy six, he had logged 1,250 hours.

The pilot requested SVFR clearance or special visible flight rules clearance -- allowing him to fly in weather conditions worse than the ones approved for ordinary apparent flight rules.

Pilots sometimes request SVFR clearance mid-flight if weather situations exchange. The ones granted permission to maintain nearer contact with air site visitors control.

Zobayan turned around till air visitors manage authorized SVFR clearance.

He resumed his adventure north approximately nine:33 a.M. PT.

The chopper flew into Burbank, after which Van Nuys airspace at 1,400 ft.

"Van Nuys, Helicopter 2EX with you for the special VFR transition," the pilot stated.

Zobayan, at one point, requested radar help to avoid traffic. The tower stated the helicopter was too low to be picked up on radar.

The pilot told controllers he changed into mountain climbing better to avoid a cloud layer.

They spoke back, however, got no reaction.

Fans are barred access to a disaster website online

Radar confirmed the helicopter climbed 2, three hundred feet, and then started a left descending flip, an NTSB legit stated.

It ignored clearing a mountain by using 20 to 30 ft. Earlier than plummeting more than 2,000 toes a minute. The conversation turned into misplaced.

Air site visitors manipulate attempted to touch the pilot again about nine: forty-two a.m. PT. No response.

"72EX, you are following a 1200 code. So you're asking for flight following?" the controller requested.

Three minutes later, the twin-engine Sikorsky S-76B fell off the radar.

The first 911 call approximately the crash was made at 9:forty seven a.M. PT -- 2 hours, 13 mins before the scheduled tip-off of the lady Mambas' sport.

The impact shattered the helicopter to pieces. The debris subject within the rugged terrain spanned 500 to six hundred ft.

At the mountainside lay the stays of nine souls, such as the super and complicated guy who once scored eighty-one factors in a single sport and 60 elements in his NBA farewell.

Lengthy a luminary on the global stage, Bryant could by no means again celebrate the NBA achievements of the subsequent technology. Or name plays for the woman Mambas. Or pray silently in a church sanctuary. Or include his wife and daughters.

The loss reverberated around the sector. La County Sheriff Deputies enforced an emergency ordinance issued as the surprise of Bryant's dying unfold. The law barred unlawful get right of entry to the crash location to stop fanatics from swarming the website.

Chapter 2

Kobe Bryant Professional career

I first found out about how a lot he cared when he confirmed up for a charity sport for storm Katrina sufferers in Houston on the 11th of September, 2005. I'm able never to direct the image of him sitting next to a younger black boy on the bench at some point in the charity occasion. Nor will I forget how he took the time to invite me questions about my New Orleans-primarily based parents and own family, who had been affected by Katrina. It meant the world to me. There have been different NBA stars there that day, which include LeBron James and Allen Iverson, but Bryant becomes the celebrity of the celebs.

I first found out about Kobe's graciousness on Oct. 24, 2008, when my former college basketball teammate Troy McCoy took his 7-year-vintage son, Cameron, and of his buddies to a la Lakers preseason game as a birthday gift. After hearing the kids cheering loudly for the Lakers in an in any other case quiet recreation, Lakers media family members director Alison Bogli gave McCoy, and the youngsters postgame passes to fulfill a few players. Long after the game, Bryant got here out of the locker room, searching around and pronouncing, "In which Cameron at? Where's Cameron?"

A stunned Cameron positioned his hand up in the air but became too shy to say anything. Kobe walked up to the boy and said, "Howdy, my name is Kobe. What's your name?" Bryant was given Cameron to respond, then presented the kids phrases of awareness and took a photograph with them.

Kobe approached among human beings; he became requested to fulfill postgame with attention to detail and recognition, just like how he played ball.

"He could do numerous due diligence on his personal," Michelle Obeso-Theus, who labored for Bryant from 2011-15, once advised The Undefeated. "Irrespective of how people view him, he is a genius very tenacious.

"He taught me willpower and sacrifice to be top-notch. His vision to peer the future was loopy. While he said he desired to fulfill someone, he continually desired to know what made them awesome. It didn't remember if they have been a wood-carver. He wanted to apprehend the mentality of what it takes for them to be a wooden-carver."

On Sunday morning, Bryant died at age forty-one in a helicopter crash in Calabasas, California, along with his 13-yr-old daughter Gianna and seven others. He leaves behind a basketball legacy as one of the finest NBA gamers of all time and one in every of its fiercest competition. He changed into an NBA MVP, 5-time champion, 18-time All-star, 11-time first group all-NBA choice, and two-time Olympic gold medalist. But he turned into so much more.

After he suffered a torn Achilles tendon damage in 2013, Bryant, showing his aggressive hearth, said thru electronic mail: "Please do me a favor although and write a piece about what I was doing before getting harm and the numbers I used to be placing up and bringing the crew to the footstep of the postseason. I sense they forget how correct I was for ANY age. And that not anything in my career indicates that I gained come lower back just as suitable or higher subsequent season."

Once more, when I mistakenly asked a query and referred to his four NBA championships, he fast corrected me — it changed into five — and gave me that Mamba glare.

Kobe often became accommodating to me while doing interviews after games and practices. He called me "huge Spears" and used to provide me a hard time for asking thought-provoking questions, once saying, "man, you always asking me the ones Dr. Seuss a– questions." He knew I might want to take his joking. Kobe had a sharp sense of humor.

One time along with his Nike proper-hand man Nico Harrison with the aid of his side, he playfully objected to interviewing with me after a Lakers exercise unless I changed my cloth wardrobe that day: an Adidas sweatsuit and footwear. Take into account that Kobe turned into then a Nike endorser who had a horrific breakup with Adidas. After a few excellent-natured ribbing, he did the interview.

But while it got here right down to it, Kobe changed into considerate. In March 2016, I landed a job because the senior NBA writer for ESPN's The Undefeated and I gave him the news through email. Bryant spoke back through writing: "happy for you, my brother!!! Write from the coronary heart!!! Usually, here for you."

On Dec. 17, 2018, I was accessible because the Lakers retired each his No. 8 and No. 24. It became his night time, but on his manner out, he caught a glimpse of me and yelled, "large Spears." We shared an include and had a brief communication earlier than he becomes whisked away. And I am some distance from the simplest reporter who Kobe changed into gracious to, as he made time for endless different media human beings in sports and past.

Adolescence

Kobe Bean Bryant was born on August 23, 1978, in Philadelphia, Pennsylvania. Named after a metropolis in Japan, Bryant is the son of former NBA participant Joe "Jellybean" Bryant.

In 1984, after ending his NBA career, the elder Bryant took the circle of relatives to Italy, in which he played within the Italian League. Developing up in Italy alongside athletic older sisters, Shaya and Sharia, Bryant becomes an avid participant of each basketball and football. When the circle of relatives again to Philadelphia in 1991, Bryant joined the decrease Merion high college basketball team, leading it to the kingdom championships four years in a row. With an eye fixed at the NBA, he additionally commenced running out with the 76ers.

Though he boasted excellent grades and excessive SAT rankings, Bryant determined to go immediately to the NBA from excessive college.

He became selected by way of the Charlotte Hornets with the 13th usual choice of the 1996 NBA draft and changed into ultimately traded to the la Lakers.

NBA career and Stats

In his 2nd season with the Lakers, Bryant changed into voted a starter for the 1998 All-megastar sport, becoming the youngest All-star in NBA records at 19. The capturing shield then teamed up with celebrity middle Shaquille O'Neal to win three consecutive NBA championships and became voted first-crew all-NBA from 2002-2004. He additionally inked multi-year endorsement offers with Adidas, Sprite, and other top sponsors.

Although the Lakers struggled after O'Neal left in 2004, Bryant carried out brilliantly. He scored eighty-one points towards the Toronto Raptors in January 2006, the second one-highest single-recreation mark in NBA records, and led the league in scoring that year and the next.

In 2008, Bryant changed into named most treasured participant and carried his team to the NBA Finals, wherein they lost to the Boston Celtics. Inside the 2009 NBA Finals, the Lakers beat the Orlando Magic to win the championship. Shortly later on, Bryant changed into a part of the memorial service to honor pal and tune celebrity, Michael Jackson. The subsequent year, the Lakers gained their 2d directly identify by using defeating the Celtics.

Bryant performed on both the 2008 and 2012 U.S. Olympic teams, winning consecutive gold medals with teammates Kevin Durant, LeBron James, and Carmelo Anthony, among several different top gamers.

After struggling a torn Achilles tendon in April 2013, Bryant labored challenging to return to the courtroom before fracturing his knee just six games into the 2013-2014 seasons. The veteran All-famous person handed Michael Jordan for 0.33 all-time on the NBA scoring list in December 2014. Still, his season ended due to damage for the 0.33 directly yr when he sustained a torn rotator cuff in January 2015.

Retirement

Although Bryant returned in time for the beginning of the 2015-2016 NBA season, he is my view struggled along with his young Lakers teammates. In November 2015, he announced that he would retire at the quilt of the season. "This season is all I've left to present," he wrote at the players' Tribune website. "My heart can take the pounding. My thoughts can handle the grind, but my frame is aware of it's time to say goodbye."

The announcement drew a strong response, especially from NBA Commissioner Adam Silver. "With 17 NBA All-celebrity alternatives, an NBA MVP, five NBA championships with the Lakers, two Olympic gold medals, and a relentless paintings ethic, Kobe Bryant is one of the greatest players inside the records of our sport," Silver stated in an assertion. "Whether or not competing within the Finals or hoisting jump pictures after the middle of the night in an empty gymnasium, Kobe has an unconditional love for the sport."

On April 13, 2016, Bryant dazzled an offered-out crowd on the Staples middle and lovers everywhere inside the ultimate sport of his profession, scoring 60 factors and leading the Lakers to a win in opposition to the Utah Jazz. It became Bryant's sixth 60-point sport of his career.

After the game, Bryant spoke to the gang. "I cannot trust how speedy two decades went by," he stated. "that is surely loopy ... And to be status at the middle courtroom with you men, my teammates in the back of me, appreciating the adventure that we've got been on — we've been via our ups, been through our downs. I assume the maximum essential element is all of us stayed collectively during."

An all-famous person lineup of Laker icons also paid tribute to Bryant, along with O'Neal, Phil Jackson, Pau Gasol, Derek Fisher, Lamar Odom, and Magic Johnson. "We're right here to celebrate greatness for two decades," Johnson stated. "Excellence for two decades. Kobe Bryant has by no means cheated the sport, never cheated us because of the fanatics. He has played via harm; he has performed hurt. And we have five championship banners to show for it."

Academy Award for 'pricey Basketball.'

In November 2015, Bryant introduced his upcoming retirement from the Lakers with a poem at the players' Tribune website, titled "Dear Basketball." The athletic brilliant quickly sought the first-rate in other fields to show his poem right into a short film, consisting of Disney animator Glen Keane and composer John Williams.

The result turned into a beautifully rendered 5-minute, 20-2nd film, which debuted at the 2017 Tribeca movie pageant. Oscar electorate took observe, leading to the unexpected sight of Bryant accepting an Academy Award for the excellent animated brief film at the 2018 rite.

The Academy of motion photograph Arts and technology's short films and animation department also prolonged an invitation for Bryant to turn out to be a member of the organization. But, in June 2018, it was revealed that the Academy's governors committee had rescinded the invitation, pronouncing the retired basketball first-rate wished to inform greater efforts inside the discipline earlier than being taken into consideration for membership.

Sexual assault fee

In July 2003, Bryant changed into charged with one depend on sexual attack on a 19-year-vintage female lodge employee in Colorado. Bryant said he changed into responsible for adultery but innocent of the rape rate. The case against Bryant changed into disregarded in 2004, and he established the civil lawsuit filed with the aid of the inn employee towards him out of court.

Philanthropy

Between his generous endeavors, the basketball amazing partnered with the non-profit After-school as a part of the Kobe & Vanessa Bryant circle of relatives foundation. He also ran an annual summer camp referred to as the Kobe Basketball School.

Kobe Bryant's circle of relatives

Kobe Bryant poses along with his daughters (L-R) Gianna, Bianka, and Natalia and wife Vanessa (left of Kobe) all through halftime after each his #eight and #24 Los Angeles Lakers jerseys are retired at Staples Middle on December 18, 2017, in la, California.

Wife and kids

Bryant married 19-12 months-antique Vanessa Laine in April 2001. The couple has become parents to four daughters: Natalia Diamante (b. 2003), Gianna Maria-Onore (b. 2006, d. 2020), Bianka (b. 2016), and Capri (b. 2019).

"We're devastated by the unexpected loss of my adoring husband, Kobe — the extraordinary father of our children; and my lovely, candy Gianna — a loving, thoughtful, and outstanding daughter, and a great sister to Natalia, Bianka, and Capri," Bryant's wife Vanessa posted on Instagram. "There aren't sufficient phrases to explain our pain right now. I take comfort in knowing that Kobe and Gigi both knew that they had been so deeply cherished. We had been so highly blessed to have them in our lives. I wish they were here with us all the time. They have been our lovely advantages taken from us too soon."

Childhood

Kobe 'Bean' Bryant becomes born on August 23, 1978, in Philadelphia, Pennsylvania. His father changed into Joe Bryant, a former Philadelphia

76ers participant. He turned into driven via his father from an early age to take in basketball. He started gambling basketball at the age of 3, and his preferred group becomes the Lakers.

When Bryant was six, his father left the NBA and moved his family to Rieti in Italy to maintain gambling expert basketball. Bryant has become conversant in his new life-style and discovered to talk fluent Italian. During summers, he would come back to America to play in a basketball summer league.

High college

Bryant earned a national reputation for the duration of a magnificent high school profession at decrease Merion high faculty placed in Ardmore, Philadelphia. He became the first freshman in decades to start to decrease Merion's varsity crew; however, the team finished with a

4-20 file. The following three years, the Aces compiled a seventy seven-thirteen report, with Bryant gambling all five positions. At some point in his junior 12 months, he averaged 31.1 points, 10. rebounds and five.2 assists and become named Pennsylvania player of the year, attracting interest from university recruiters within the system. Duke, Michigan, North Carolina, and Villanova had been on the pinnacle of his listing; but, while Kevin Garnett went inside the first spherical of the 1995 NBA draft, he started out considering going without delay to the professionals.

Adjusting to the NBA

Bryant opted to forgo college and declared him eligible for the NBA draft when he graduated from excessive school. The Charlotte Hornets chose him with the 13th pick out of the 1996 draft. He turned into traded to the Lakers rapidly after that and became the second one youngest NBA participant in history while the 1996-ninety seven seasons opened. He quickly proved his advantage with the Lakers and turned into selected for the NBA All-celebrity sport in just his second season, turning into the youngest all-megastar.

Three-peat

Bryant becomes compelled to share the function of the Lakers' megastar player, along with his famous and talented teammate Shaquille O'Neal. The 2 had an uneasy relationship, but they found fulfillment below the management of Phil Jackson, who became train of the Lakers in 1999. Bryant, taking pictures to protect, and O'Neal, a center, meshed right into a remarkably effective aggregate, and, by the point, Bryant was 23, the Lakers had gained three consecutive NBA championships.

Championships

Although the Lakers struggled after O'Neal left in 2004, Bryant executed brilliantly. He scored eighty-one factors towards the Toronto Raptors in January 2006, the second-maximum single-sport mark in NBA history, and led the league in scoring that year and the subsequent.

In 2008, Bryant became named maximum precious participant and carried his crew to the NBA Finals, where they lost to the Boston Celtics. Within the 2009 NBA Finals, the Lakers beat the Orlando Magic to win the championship. Rapidly in a while, Bryant was a part of the memorial provider to honor buddy and music celebrity Michael Jackson. The subsequent year, the Lakers received their second direct name by using defeating the Celtics.

Career ranking

Career – season

- (33,643) Points – 4th
- Attempts (26,200) Field goal – 3rd
- Made (11,719) Field goals– 5th
- Missed (14,481) Field goals– 1st
- made (8,378) Free throws – 3rd
- attempts (10,011) Free throw– 5th
- (25.00) Points per game – 12th
- attempts (5,546) 3-point field goal– 6th
- (4,010) Turnovers – 3rd
- made (1,827) 3-point field goals– 12th
- 14th (1,944) Steals
- (48,637) Minutes played – 6th
- (1.44) Steals per game – 92nd
- (36.13) Minutes per game – 41st
- (1,346) Games played – 11th –

- 29th (6,306) Assists –
- (.8369) Free throw % – 84th
- (3,353) Personal fouls – 39th
- (5,548) Defensive rebounds – 46th
- (4.69) Assists per game – 134th
- (7,047) Rebounds – 100th
- (640) Blocks – 180th
- (1,499) Offensive rebounds – 190th

Career – playoffs

- (882) 3-point field goal attempts – 3rd
- (292) 3-point field goals made – 6th
- (4,499) Field goal attempts – 3rd
- (1,320) Free throws made – 3rd
- (5,640) Points – 4th
- (8,641) Minutes played – 3rd
- (647) Turnovers – 3rd
- (66,014) Field goals made – 5th

NBA awards and accomplishments

- 5-time: 2000, 2001, 2002, 2009, 2010 NBA champion
- 7 NBA: 2000, 2001, 2002, 2004, 2008, 2009, 2010 Finals appearances
- 2-time N: 2009, 2010 BA Finals MVP
- NBA: 2008 Most Valuable Player
- 2-time: 2006, 2007 scoring champion
- 18-time: 1998, 2000, 2001, 2002, 2003, 2004, 2005, 2006, 2007, 2008, 2009, 2010, 2011, 2012, 2013, 2014, 2015, 2016 NBA All-Star
- 4-time: 2002, 2007, 2009, 2011 (shared the 2009 award with Shaquille O'Neal) NBA All-Star Game MVP
- Team selection All-NBA: 15-time

- First team: 2002- 2003-2004-2006-2007-2008-2009-2010, 2011-2012-2013
- Second team: 2000-2001
- 1999-2005 Third team:
- 12-time Team- selection: All-Defensive
- First team: 2000-2003-2004-2006-.2007-2008-2009-2010-2011
- Second team: 2001-2002-2012
- Awarded separately Player of the Month to Eastern and Western Conference 2001–2002.
- Regular season leader: NBA
- 1998–99 (50), 2007–08 (82), 2008–09 (82) Games played
- 2005–06 (38.7), 2010–11 (35.1), 2011–12 (35.7) Practice percentage:
- points: 2002–03 (2,461), 2005–06 (2,832, 7th in NBA history), 2006–07 (2,430), 2007–08 (2,323)

- 2006–07 (31.6) Points per game: 2005–06 (35.4, 8th in NBA history),
- Attempted field goals: 2005–06 (2,173), 2006–07 (1,757), 2007–08 (1,690), 2010–11 (1,639), 2011–12 (1336)
- 2002–03 (868), 2005–06 (978), 2006–07 (813) made field goals
- 2006–07 (768) attempted: free throws
- 2005–06 (696), 2006–07 (667) made:free throws
- 81 (on January 22, 2006 vs. the Toronto Raptors) in a game: 2nd most points
- 2x Best NBA Player 2008, 2010 ESPY Award winner:
- playoffs leader NBA:
- 2001 (3.8) win shares:
- 2004 -(539), 2008 -(633), 2009 -(695), 2010 -(671) points:
- 2003 (32.1), 2007 (32.8), 2008 (30.1) per game points

- 2002 (833), 2004 (973) played minutes
- 2004 (190), 2008 (222), 2009 (242), 2010 (234) made field goals
- 2002 (431), 2004 (460), 2008 (463), 2009 (530), 2010 (511) attempted field goals
- 2004 (135), 2008 (157), 2009 (174), 2010 (154) made free throws
- 2008 (194), 2010 (183) attempted free throws
- 2000 (32), 2009 (38) steals
- 2010 (79) turnovers
- 2000 (89) personal fouls

NBA records

Currently holds

NBA records: Bryant holds

- For a single 20 maximum Seasons performed (tied with Dirk Nowitzki) NBA Franchise

- Game MVP awards won: four (tied with Bob Pettit) most All-superstar

- All-superstar sport maximum offensive rebounds in an: 10

- Maximum All-NBA total alternatives gained, career: 15 (tied with Kareem Abdul-Jabbar and Tim Duncan)

- First group honors received, career: 11 All-NBA

- First-team honors received, profession: 9 (tied with Michael Jordan, Gary Payton, and Kevin Garnett) All-defensive

- Four-sport playoff collection: fifty-one (2d round vs. Sacramento Kings, 2001) most free throws made

- Sixteen,161 (as of April 14, 2016, at Staples middle, Los Angeles) scored in a single arena, profession

- Profession: 599 (as of April 14, 2016, at Staples middle, la maximum games played at one arena

- Towards relaxation of groups in the league above 40 (proportion with Bob Pettit) highest score

- The preceding holder of the report surpassed Hakeem Olajuwon

- Youngest participant to attain 32,000 points: (36 years, 87 days)

- surpassed Karl Malone, the previous holder of the document

- Youngest participant to attain 33,000 factors: (37 years, 138 days)

- exceeded Kareem Abdul-Jabbar, the previous holder of the report

- Youngest participant to be named to the NBA All-Rookie crew: (1996–ninety-seven)

- Youngest player to be named to the NBA All-defensive crew: (1999–00)

- Youngest player to begin a recreation: (18 years, 158 days)

- Youngest player to win the: (18 years, 169 days) NBA Slam Dunk Championship

- All-superstar recreation: (19 years, 169 days) Youngest participant to begin

- Within the postseason score at least six hundred factors only player in NBA history for three serial years

- 633 -(2008)-695- (2009)-671 (2010)

- Oldest participant,: (37 years, 234 days) score 60+ points

Kobe Bryant's legendary NBA career summed up in 8 eye-popping stats

Kobe Bryant's NBA career doubles as a list of some of basketball's most astounding accomplishments.

33,583 career ordinary-season factors. 26, a hundred and fifty ordinary-season shot tries. 16 All-NBA teams. A franchise-report 20 seasons with the la Lakers sadly, over two hundred video games neglected because of injury and, of the path, the ones five vibrant jewelry.

Those are some of the extra heralded numbers from Kobe's gambling time, but they're a long way from alone. To have a good time the destiny hall of Famer, we dove deep and came up with a number of the more absurd, off-the-wall numbers that we may want to come up with — as well as some which you probably already recognize.

Right here, then, are the eight pieces of information that outline Kobe Bryant's NBA career.

1,056,976: Approximate variety of miles Kobe has traveled via plane in his 20 seasons

We went via all two decades of Bryant's sport logs and traced his approximate tour direction from one game to the subsequent, together with the All-big name ruin and playoffs (we did no longer include the preseason, because might be silly). We used the foremost metropolitan airport in every NBA city to degree space — an imperfect size, admittedly, however, a first-rate proxy was given the sheer wide variety of miles we're talking approximately.

And the result is remarkable. Bryant has flown sufficient miles to make it to the moon and again twice with a few rooms to spare. 2009-10 was the most jetlag-inducing season for Kobe, as the Lakers traveled about 80,000 miles at some stage in their championship season. Within the seasons that weren't shortened via lockout or Bryant damage, Kobe averaged about 60,000 miles within the air consistent with year.

518: 30-point games in Kobe's career

Bryant topped 30 factors in over one out of every three video games he performed in the course of his profession permit that sink in because it's sincerely ridiculous. That's 14 extra than Kareem Abdul-Jabbar had — and nonetheless 153 fewer than Michael Jordan.

1,810: general wide variety of NBA players who played at least one minute over the last 20 seasons

There are most effective approximately 450 roster spots within the league in any given 12 months, and every season brought a mean of ninety new players into the fold. Most played fewer than 100 mins.

36: instances Kobe hit a sport-winner

The Lakers received 970 games inside the regular season and playoffs with Kobe in the courtroom.

Almost four percent of these wins came courtesy of a closing-2nd shot from the Black Mamba.

89.3: percentage of Kobe's profession spent with Shaquille O'Neal, Phil Jackson, Pau Gasol

Kobe haters will usually point to the considerable quantity of skills he was surrounded by with the Lakers.

However it one way or the other looks like Bryant played a miles large portion of his profession without his "huge three" than this — in all likelihood because that 2004-05 season lasted a damn lifetime.

Seventy-two: gamers in NBA records who've attempted as many pictures as Kobe missed within the regular season

Shooters must shoot. It's what they do. And headed into his final game on Wednesday, Bryant has neglected 14,435 shots inside the ordinary season.

Kobe Bryant's Stats, Highlights, and Reaction from Final NBA Game

Kobe Bryant referred to as it quits Wednesday night time in a way only he could.

While the Los Angeles Lakers seemed destined for a loss to the Utah Jazz inside the very last game of the Black Mamba's ancient 20-year NBA career, Bryant cooked up a signature performance for the a while as he dropped 60 points on 50 photographs to hand the pink and gold a hundred and one-96 win at a raucous Staples middle.

The 60-factor game changed into the 6th of Bryant's career, and it left LeBron James in awe:

Bryant's 60-point explosion turned into additionally the highest-scoring recreation within the NBA all season, and he broke Michael Jordan's unmarried-game subject-aim try document inside the method, in line with Basketball-Reference.Com.

In an antique performance that conjured up reminiscences of his glory days, Bryant's commitment to extend scoring and taking pictures served as a wonderful tribute to the style of play that ingratiated him to fans over the past couple of many years.

Kobe's final game wouldn't have been whole without some sit back-inducing pregame tributes, and the Lakers pulled out all the stops to shower one of the franchise's true legends with the reward he deserved.

From montages along with former teammates and NBA luminaries to Laker legend Magic Johnson calling Kobe "the best to put on the purple and gold" during a special in-individual presentation, in step with the Orange County sign in's invoice Oram, the festivities seemed to sincerely touch Kobe as he watched from the bench earlier than making his way to middle courtroom.

With an enduring legacy that consists of 5 titles, a 3rd-place perch on the all-time scoring listing, one everyday-season MVP, two Finals MVPs and a spotlight reel complete of signature moments that may activate nostalgia in seconds, Bryant can walk away knowing he cemented his region as one of the maximum dominant and precise players the sport will ever see.

  With an enduring legacy that consists of 5 titles, a third-vicinity perch at the all-time scoring listing, one everyday-season MVP, two Finals

MVPs and a spotlight reel full of signature moments which can spark off nostalgia in seconds, Bryant can walk away understanding he cemented his area as one of the most dominant and particular gamers the sport will ever see.

"I respect the adventure we've been on USA and downs ... I suppose the most vital part is all of us stayed collectively all through," Bryant stated, per Trudell.

Chapter 3

Kobe Bryant's most inspirational quotes

Kobe Bryant turned into certainly one of 9 human beings killed in a helicopter crash on Sunday. He turned into 41. His thirteen-12 months-vintage daughter Gianna becomes also killed in the crash.

Bryant turned into one of the finest NBA players of all-time and an icon within the sports activities world. Further to his fulfillment on the basketball court docket, Bryant changed into acknowledged for a ceaseless work ethic and awesome power.

In honor of Bryant's legacy, right here are 11 inspiring charges from Bryant on tough paintings, fulfillment, and lifestyles.

Kobe Bryant on achieving achievement:

"While you make a desire and say, 'Come hell or excessive water, I am going to be this,' then you have not to be surprised while you are that. It has to be now not intoxicating or out of person due to the fact you have visible this second for a goodbye that while that second comes, of the direction it's miles here. After all, it has been right here the whole time because it has been [in your mind] the whole time."

His recommendation to Gordon Hayward about returning rehabbing damage:

"Reality offers nothing returned and no need to you. Time to transport on and recognition on doing everything to your energy to put together for surgical procedure, ask all of the questions to be sure you understand the manner so you might also visualize it on your unconscious while being operated on and higher the risk of it is success then attention on the healing procedure each day using day. It's an extended adventure; however, in case your attention at the mini-milestones alongside the manner you'll discover splendor within the conflict of doing easy things that before this damage were taken for granted. This could also imply that when you return, you'll have a new attitude. You will be so appreciative of being able to stand, walk, run that you may educate more difficult than you ever have. You notice the perception within you develop with every mini-milestone, and you may come a better player for it again."

At the mission of coming back from accidents:

"The method of it [drives me to come back]. I want to see if I'm able to. I do not know if I will. I need to discover. I want to peer. I'm going to do what I continually do: I'm going to break it down to its smallest form, smallest detail, and pass after it. Each day, in the future at a time."

Ongoing straight from high school to the NBA:

"I want to discover ways to come to be the great basketball player inside the globe. And if I am going to examine that, I got study from the first-rate. Kids go to high school to be medical doctors or attorneys, so forth and so forth, and that is in which they observe. My area to observe is from satisfactory."

On figuring out, he changed into specific from other NBA gamers:

"I by no means looked at [basketball] as work. I didn't recognize it become work until my first year in the NBA. Once I got here round, I was surrounded by different professionals and that I concept basketball was going to be the whole lot to them, and it wasn't. And I was like, 'this is distinctive.' I idea everybody became so obsessive approximately the sport like me. It became like, no? Oh, this is difficult work. I am getting it now."

On failure:

"When we're pronouncing this cannot be accomplished, this can't be finished, then we're brief-converting ourselves. My brain cannot cause technique failure. It'll now not a system failure. Due to the fact if I have to take a seat there and face myself and tell myself, 'you are a failure,' I suppose that is worse, that is nearly worse than demise."

On no longer being scared of failure:

"I don't mean to sound cavalier after I say that, however never. It is basketball. I've practiced and practiced and performed so normally. There may be nothing clearly to be afraid of, while you consider it ... Due to the fact I have failed earlier than, and that I awakened the subsequent morning, and I am good enough. Human beings say terrible things approximately you within the paper on Monday, and then on Wednesday, you are the finest factor because sliced bread. I've visible that cycle, so why could I be anxious approximately it happening?"

On making sacrifices:

"There's a desire that we have to make as people. If you want to be tremendous at something, there's a preference you have to make. We can all be masters at our craft; however, you have to make a preference. What I mean with the aid of this is, there are inherent sacrifices that come alongside that — own family time, putting out along with your pals, being a first-rate friend. Being a top-notch son, nephew, regardless of the case, can be. Some sacrifices come alongside that."

On what it takes to steer:

"leadership is lonely ... I'm no longer going to be terrified of disagreement to get us to wherein we want to head. There's a large false impression in which human beings are thinking prevailing or achievement comes from all and sundry setting their hands around every different and making a song kumbaya and patting them at the lower back when they reduce to rubble, and that is now not fact. If you are going to be a pacesetter, you are not going to delight every person. You have to hold humans responsible even if you have that moment of being uncomfortable."

On prevailing his first championship:

"I will consider triumphing the primary championship and form of being like, 'ok, now what? What occurs now?' ... [Teammates] celebrating, waving champagne bottles around ... And out of doors of that, it becomes, 'k, now what?'"

On retiring and facing the stop of his basketball career:

"There's splendor in that. I suggest it is going through the cycle. I suggest it is the cycle; this is the herbal progression of boom, of maturation. I suggest there may be no disappointment in that ... I see the beauty in now not being capable of blow beyond defenders anymore, and you recognize what I mean? I see the beauty in getting up in the morning and being in pain due to the fact I recognize all the hard work that it took to get to this point. So, I am no longer, and I'm not sad about it. I'm very appreciative of what I have had."

Chapter 4

The Kobe Bryant Guide to Life: Inspirational Tips to Become More Successful

Kobe Bryant is someone who will stay on for generations to return. He turned into drafted from high school and is considered one of the fine basketball players to have ever played the sport. Throughout his existence, he labored noticeably difficult to be a hit and wonderful basketball player, great father, and standard a top-notch individual.

He described himself using the phrase "mamba mentality," and he once stated,

Stop feeling sorry for yourself, discover the silver lining, and get to paintings with the identical notion, equal force, and identical conviction as ever. Someday, the start of a brand new professional adventure will commence. These days are not that day. 'in case you see me in combat with a bear, prey for the undergo.' I've constantly cherished that quote. That's 'mamba mentality' we don't give up, we don't cower, we don't run. We bear and overcome.

Kobe's success turned into due to the mentality he followed. Here are seven hints stimulated by Kobe, on how to become extra a success.

Pointers to emerge as more a hit:

1. Kobe's IQ

Kobe Bryant has arguably the best basketball IQ within the NBA. He changed into one of the maxima technically sound gamers in the whole sport. On every occasion, he changed into at the court docket, he becomes continually one step ahead of his opposition. What does this have to do with fulfillment? Properly in life, understanding is power. The greater, the better you could put together. If you are privy to your environment and can stay one step ahead of your colleagues. You may have a facet over others and could significantly boom your chances of turning into a hit.

You need to:

Pay attention extra than you talk. You'll be amazed by way of how plenty extra you analyze

Ask for remarks and examine it.

Growth your avenue smarts or social IQ.

2. Kobe's flexible Offense game

There weren't loads missing from Kobe's offensive arsenal. He would take that long three, pull up over you in the publish, or even power it down the lane for a sweet dunk. How does this follow to fulfillment? Nicely, in place of simplest shooting from one spot, you have to discover ways to force, take a layup, or even dunk.

You need to learn how to become multifaceted and enlarge your opportunities. Attempt new matters and don't turn out to be slim-minded. It's simply common sense. The greater wells that you dig, the better your probabilities become of hitting the water. But usually understand that one nicely absolutely dug is better than one hundred wells dug the simplest midway. So even as you should try unique ways to become a success, ensure that for each manner you try, you do it to the excellent of your abilities.

3. Kobe's work Ethic

Kobe Bryant had an unequaled work ethic when it comes to basketball. While he was proficient in his abilities, he advanced on himself day by day, and his difficult paintings were what lead him to emerge as who he becomes. As an instance, he used to expose up for practice at 5 AM and leave at 7 PM in high faculty! This force applies at once to anybody who desires to come to be a hit. And if you're nonetheless now not convinced, test out this tale with the aid of considered one of his trainers: Kobe's paintings-Ethic. Difficult paintings and achievement move hand to hand. You couldn't have one without the opposite. As Kobe once said:

"I've nothing unusual with lazy people who blame others for his or her loss of achievement. Tremendous matters come from difficult work and perseverance. No excuses."

4. Kobe's Sub-zero Blood

Kobe Bryant changed into the definition of cold-blooded. I imply there's a cause they known as him the Black Mamba. The taunts of the gang or the mind video games that the other players played, simply didn't paintings on him. He continually remained cool, calm, and collected. While it might be time to strike, he might strike hard and silence arenas. His potential to dam out the noise is what helped him to enhance himself, and this capacity is something you must attend to turn out to be successful.

You need to learn how to use all the bad electricity around you and convert it into choice and motivation to prevail. There will constantly be haters and those who come within the way of your desires; however, you need to push upward and live targeted in your goal and success.

5. Kobe's willpower

Kobe tracked goals like they were his prey. Once he determined to reach them, he doesn't allow something to stand his manner. He had proven this at some point in his profession, particularly while he again from ACL damage in advance of schedule at the age of 34. His "I'm going to get it" attitude is what you should do away with if you need to come to be a hit.

You must be making desires and dominating them on an everyday basis. You must have mini-dreams inside your normal desires, and then ordinary desires inner of your bigger dreams.

Fulfillment is a goal-primarily based beast, and also you ought to feed it.

6. Kobe's Social Portfolio

I wager numerous you don't realize this; however, Kobe changed into a networking Guru. Inside the previous few years, he had spread his name no longer simply inside the West; however, even in the East and through the energy of social media, he had, without a doubt, emerge as a worldwide icon. You must put emphasis specifically on his capacity to the community.

You ought to:

Try and expand your non-public community by using assisting others while they may be in need.

Create as a good deal as connections as you may because you in no way know when anyone may are available in handy.

7. Kobe's capability to conform

Kobe had reinvented himself in the course of his career. Inside the early ranges of his profession, Kobe used to be a slashing, high flying shooting guard who used to dunk with authority. Once he reached an older age, toward the top of his career, he has become an agile, rapid capturing shield with a light touch.

Those are both completely distinctive playing styles but also are the correct kind for each time. To emerge as a success, you should have this potential to evolve the interior of you. You ought to be able to read the frame language of the people around you and adapt and change as a result.

Final phrases

I'm chasing perfection. – Kobe Bryant

I would love to thank Kobe for uplifting so many individuals globally (along with myself!). He truly became an extremely good participant to be well-remembered. His determination and power are what he hoped to teach everyone around him.

Kobe Bryant: His most inspiring quotes on life and basketball

News of Kobe Bryant's passing on Sunday maintains to bring unhappiness to all people who loved and adored him.

The Los Angeles Lakers legend and his daughter, Gianna, had been tragically killed along with seven others in a helicopter crash in California.

Wearing icons inclusive of Michael Jordan, Cristiano Ronaldo, and Tiger Woods have all paid tribute to the late forty one-12 months-old and some of his best moments are being shared throughout social media.

It is, despite everything, as lots of time to rejoice Bryant's legacy in life and recreation as a whole lot as its miles to mourn his passing.

And inside the wake of the tragic news, folks who seemed as much as Bryant have shared some of his most inspiring rates to expose what the double-Olympic champion supposed to them.

There may be no thinking that Bryant's dedication to his craft made him a remarkable role version as well as his work far from the courtroom and campaigning for ladies' recreation.

As a result, we have decided to raise a pitcher to Bryant's legacy with the aid of looking through eleven of his maximum inspiring costs to celebrate everything he stood for across his forty-one years in the world.

1. On lifestyles itself

"Have an excellent time. Lifestyles are just too brief to get bogged down and be discouraged. You need to maintain shifting. You have to hold going. Put one foot in the front of the opposite, smile, and keep on rolling."

2. on achieving success

"When you make a preference and say, 'Come hell or excessive water, I am going to be this,' you then should now not be surprised when you are that.

"It needs to no longer be intoxicating or out of person because you've got visible this second for a goodbye that ... While that second comes, of the direction, it's miles right here as it has been right here the whole time, as it has been [in your mind] the complete time."

3. Ongoing directly from school to the NBA

"I need to discover ways to become the best basketball participant inside the international. And if I am going to research that, I got study from the fine.

"Youngsters pass to high school to be medical doctors or legal professionals, so forth and so on, and that's in which they examine. My place to take a look at is from the first-class."

4. On being criticized for his style of play

"I've shot too much from the time I was eight years vintage. However, 'too much' is an issue of perspective? A few humans notion Mozart had too many notes in his compositions.

"Allow me placed it this manner: I entertain those who say I shoot too much. I find it very exciting. Going lower back to Mozart, he responded to critics by using saying there have been neither too many notes or too few. There have been as many as vital."

5. on comparisons to Michael Jordan

"When I have got the threat to defend Michael Jordan, I need to defend him. I need him. It's the last challenge. I don't want to be the following Michael Jordan; I most effective need to be Kobe Bryant."

6. On striving for greatness

"There's a preference that we must make as humans, as individuals. If you want to be awesome at something, there's a preference you have to make.

"All of us can be masters at our craft, but you need to make a choice. What I suggest by that is, there are inherent sacrifices that come at the side of that.

7. On coming back from accidents

"The process of it [drives me to come back]. I need to look if I'm able to. I don't know if I'm able to. I need to discover. I want to see it. I'm going to do what I constantly do: I'm going to break it all the way down to its smallest form, smallest element, and move after it. Day by day, one day at a time."

8. On triumphing

"I will do something it takes to win games, whether it's sitting on a bench waving a towel, handing a cup of water to a teammate, or hitting the game-prevailing shot."

9. On failure

"When we're announcing this cannot be achieved, this cannot be completed, then we're brief-changing ourselves. My brain, it can't afford technique failure. It's going to no longer procedure failure.

"because if I have to sit down there and face myself and inform myself, 'you are a failure,' I suppose that could be worse, that is almost worse than dying."

10. On being a pacesetter

"Management is lonely... I'm now not going to be terrified of the war of words to get us to where we need to go.

"There's a large misconception where humans questioning prevailing or fulfillment comes from anyone putting their fingers around each different and making a song kumbaya and patting them on the back when they reduce to rubble, and that's not the truth.

11. on teamwork

"The crucial component is that your teammates have to understand you are pulling for them, and you need them to be successful."

BASKET-NBA-BRYANT-dying-PHI

A person is by no means a measure of what number oft-shirt-worthy charges he can provide, however, permit all these nuggets of understanding function the ultimate evidence that Bryant's legacy will stay lengthy beyond the person himself.

Kobe Bryant's first-class costs about life

The overdue basketball first-rate stimulated lovers both on and stale the courtroom, along with his enduring skills for the game and his understanding about overcoming obstacles. In what's the notion of being his very last sit down-

down interview, published just three days before his premature loss of life, he informed the United States nowadays, "you bought to do what you like to do. I like telling stories."

Here are seven other memorable charges from Bryant's interviews over the years.

On accomplishing a tranquil thoughts

In a 2013 ESPN interview, Bryant becomes advised he regarded exclusive — he seemed calm.

"due to the fact I am. That's simply the maturation. That's 17 years of seeing everything the game can dish out. I've seen it all earlier than. There's no need to get too loopy or bent out of shape. There are nevertheless demanding situations every day. But I'm still having fun. I used to be born to play this sport. I still adore it."

On friendship

From a 2015 profile in GQ: "I have 'like minds.' I've been lucky to play in Los Angeles, and wherein there are numerous people like me. Actors, Musicians Businessmen, Obsessives. Folks that experience like God placed them on this planet to do anything it's miles that they do. Now, can we have time to build exceptional relationships? Can we have time to construct extraordinary friendships? No. Will we have time to socialize and to hang around aimlessly? No. Will we need to do that? No. We need to work. I revel in operating."

On perseverance

In a 2008 interview, he spoke to his high-quality attitude. "Have an amazing time. Existence is too brief to get slowed down and be discouraged. You have to hold shifting. You have to preserve going.

On the impossibility of perfection

In the same GQ profile, Bryant turned into asked whether or not the traits that make him high-quality also are troubles.

"Oh, yeah. However, the matters that make someone common also are problems. The things that make a person not excellent at whatever at all are a problem. In case you need to be the best of all-time at something, there's going to be a negative facet to that. In case you need to be an excessive school important, that's pleasant, too — but to also carry terrible luggage."

On preparing for surgical operation

He captioned a 2017 Instagram publish: "Be sad. Be mad. Be pissed off. Scream. Cry. Sulk. While you awaken, you may assume it was just a nightmare best to recognize it's all too real. You'll be angry and desire for the day lower back, the game again THAT play again. However, reality gives not anything lower back and no need to you."

On making sacrifices for a dream

In Showtime and CBS Sports activities' 2015 documentary "Kobe Bryant's Muse," he pondered: "all of us may be masters at our craft, but you have to make a choice. What I mean via this is, there are inherent sacrifices that come alongside that. Family time, putting out with buddies, being an extraordinary friend, being a super son, nephew, regardless of the case can be. Some sacrifices come alongside making that decision."

On failure

In "Muse," he additionally stated: "While we are announcing this cannot be done, this cannot be accomplished, then we are brief-changing ourselves. My mind, it cannot afford manner failure. It'll no longer procedure failure. Due to the fact if I ought to sit there and face myself and inform myself, 'You're a failure,' I assume that is worse, that is nearly worse than death."

More than a number: College players tell their stories about Kobe Bryant inspiring them to wear No. 24

There are 181 gamers in men's Division I basketball who wears No. 24. So a lot of them accomplish that in big component, if now not totally, because of Kobe Bryant. They arrive from greater than 30 states and ten nations, such as the Netherlands, Ukraine, Nigeria, Latvia, France, and Portugal. Australia, too. They are as quick as five-foot-10 and as tall as 7 ft.

Bryant's have an impact on over basketball, and the sports world has been overwhelming in the wake of the tragedy that took the destiny hall of Famer, his 13-year-antique daughter Gianna and seven others aboard the superstar-crossed helicopter flight on Jan. 26. Bryant retired in 2016. He played just long enough to have an idol-like effect on dozens and maybe even loads of contemporary college gamers. Under, eleven gamers who wear Bryant's No. 24 are spotlighted. They informed CBS sports activities their motives for wearing No. 24 (via rule, university players cannot wear No. Eight, the other variety Bryant wore) and what Bryant still method to them. Fees have been edited for clarity and conciseness.

Sacred heart junior E.J. Anosike (East Orange, New Jersey)

Anosike (15.7 ppg, 11.1 rpg) is arguably the great participant inside the Northeast convention and is attempting to guide Sacred coronary heart to its first NCAA match in college records. Making his veneration even stronger, Anosike's sister, Nicky, is 12 years his senior. She performed for Pat Summitt at Tennessee, and then spent five seasons in the WNBA, together with a season in l. A. With the Sparks.

"It started when I was sincerely younger, around two years vintage. He has always been my preferred participant. At the time, he turned into wearing no. Eight and I am the 8th baby, the youngest of 8 youngsters. Even if I used to be young, I ought to tell you every player on the crew. I like Kobe Bryant. My mother got me a Kobe jersey at that age. I constantly gravitated in the direction of basketball, and as I was given older, my sister might play within the WNBA, and he or she would tell me how Kobe changed into as someone and his work ethic, how he supported girls' basketball. As I started taking basketball more critically, I used to be attracted to his paintings ethic."

His first summer season at Sacred coronary heart, Anosike's coach informed players they had to make 10,000 pictures for the summertime.

Anosike insisted on taking a Kobe-like approach: he made double that -- and double everybody at the team. The subsequent summer season, he upped it to 25,000, persisted again closing summertime, and estimates he is made more than 100,000 shots on his own time.

"Constant paintings ethic, preserve getting higher and seeking to master my craft. I used to be born in New York, but I used to be raised in New Jersey. I come from a single-discern household; my mother raised all eight folks by herself. The percentages were stacked in opposition to us. Kobe, the odds were stacked him. The Celtics had the huge 3. He determined a manner to win the title. Shaq left, he observed a manner to win. As I was given to the college, I started out listening to him more and how he got to that level and the way he was given to be one of the exceptional gamers ever. I desired to be a starter, one of the pleasant gamers on the team, the satisfactory participant in the convention."

After gaining knowledge of Bryant's demise, Anosike got a name from friends back in Jersey who specialize in designs and artwork on shoes. He plans on unveiling his unique pair of Kobe tribute shoes later this month.

"Before, I wore 24 because I used to be a Kobe fan who renowned him. Each person had their motives for his or her love for Kobe. Now, I embody the range even extra because of what it symbolizes. Twenty-four hours an afternoon, you need to be centered on your grind. Now I experience like it is quite a number -- when people have a look at me, like, 'He needs to be accurate.' You don't just put on that wide variety. It's similar to the Michael Jordan effect returned in the '90s. He needs to be precise to wear that wide variety. Every day, I must convey it to show to myself, to show to all of us that I am the great and need to be the nice."

Creighton junior Mitch Ballock (Eudora, Kansas)

They won 77-66. The large moment came while Ballock hit a scramble three-pointer. He released the shot with 8 seconds left at the shot clock -- and eight:24 to go within the half.

Kobe Bryant become A Basketball massive

Kobe Bryant and his 13-yr-vintage daughter, Gianna, had been killed on Sunday morning in Calabasas, California, in a helicopter crash that still claimed the lives of the seven others on board, consistent with reviews Sunday night on this growing tale. Bryant was forty-one and is survived with the aid of his wife, Vanessa, and his three different daughters.

The NBA legend was feted with the aid of many on Saturday night for the duration of a nationally televised sport among the Philadelphia 76ers and the Los Angeles Lakers, with whom Bryant spent his whole 20-year gambling career. It changed into a celebration of the careers of Bryant and LeBron James, who handed Bryant in the course of the sport for 0.33 region at the NBA's career scoring list.

The six-foot-six capturing protect turned into one of the maximum dominant gamers on the courtroom in NBA records, racking up five NBA titles, a record 18 directly All-megastar game choices, and four All-megastar recreation MVP Awards. Bryant's legacy of the court docket is equally fantastic, with file income for an NBA participant, winning investments, and a wealthy shoe deal that driven his net worth north of $six hundred million.

Athletes and basketball fanatics around the world took to social media to percentage their emotions on Bryant. Michael Jordan, with whom Bryant changed into regularly in comparison throughout his profession, issued an assertion through his commercial enterprise manager at the tragedy: "I am in shock over the tragic information of Kobe's and Gianna's passing. Phrases can't describe the pain I'm feeling. I cherished Kobe—he turned into like a bit brother to me. We used to talk frequently, and I can leave out one's conversations very lots. He was a fierce competitor, one of the greats of the game and a creative pressure. Kobe turned into also a notable dad who loved his own family deeply—and took superb satisfaction in his daughter's love of basketball. Yvette joins me in sending our innermost condolences to Vanessa, the Lakers agency, and basketball fans around the world."

Bryant turned into born in 1978 in Philadelphia but spent a lot of his childhood in Italy, where his father, Joe "Jellybean" Bryant, performed expert basketball. He back to Philadelphia for excessive school and gained countrywide attention for his basketball prowess. He entered the NBA Draft instantly from excessive faculty at 17 years antique, at the time only the second one player to make the bounce over the previous 20 years, joining Kevin Garnett.

The Charlotte Hornets selected Bryant 13th within the 1996 NBA Draft, but a change had already been organized to deliver the Bryant choose to the Lakers, with whom he signed a three-12 months agreement for $three.5 million.

A 21-yr-old Bryant landed on the quilt of Forbes in 2000, armed with a brand new six-year, $71 million playing agreement and endorsement offers with Adidas, Mattel, Sprite, Spalding and Giorgio Armani. "Basketball was the common denominator," he said approximately growing up in Italy. "at the court, I ought to communicate." Three months later, he won the primary of 3 instantly NBA titles with Shaquille O'Neal, his co-big name in Lakers pink and gold.

Bryant became the difficulty of a sexual assault criticism filed through a 19-12 months-antique motel employee in Colorado in 2003. Bryant, who had married Vanessa two years earlier, said the come upon becoming consensual. Prosecutors dropped the expenses while the accuser refused to testify at trial. Bryant and the accuser settled a civil in shape privately, and he recounted, "I now understand how she feels that she did no longer consent to this stumble upon."

McDonald's and Nutella dropped Bryant as an endorser, but Nike, which had signed Bryant to a 4-year, $forty million deal just earlier than the accusation, caught by way of him. His Nike signature shoes might rank the various NBA's pinnacle dealers over the next 15 years and helped Nike build a $6 billion commercial enterprise in China, where Bryant changed into idolized for his capability on the court docket and his willingness to include Chinese culture.

He made annual summertime pilgrimages to China to marketplace Nike earlier than it turned into commonplace for stars to do so and turned into arguably the maximum popular athlete on the 2008 summer Olympics in Beijing. His jersey turned into often the NBA's bestseller in China, and he landed China-unique endorsements with Mercedes-Benz, smart car, and Alibaba.

Bryant, like fellow worldwide superstars Serena Williams, James, and Kevin Durant, used his massive platform while nevertheless an energetic athlete to increase his business hobbies. He installation Kobe Inc. In 2013 and told Forbes on time, "Kobe Inc.'s mission statement is to own and develop brands and ideas that task and redefine the sports activities enterprise while inspiring the arena."

The first investment for Kobe Inc. was in rising sports activities drink Body Armor. He received extra than 10% of the organization for roughly $5 million. "The version has usually been for entertainers to get sweat equity. However, I desired to develop past that," Bryant stated.

The investment had become a slam dunk when Coca-Cola invested $300 million within the startup in 2018, pushing the value of Bryant's stake to $two hundred million.

Bryant retired in 2016 with $680 million in general profits from playing salary and endorsements. It changed into the best overall ever recorded through a group athlete for the duration of their playing career.

Months after his retirement, he unveiled his $100 million assignment-capital funds, in a partnership with entrepreneur Jeff Stibel, to put money into media, era, and information corporations. Their portfolio consists of media internet site The players Tribune, video game fashion designer Scopely and prison-services corporation Legal Zoom.

Bryant frequently pointed out his love of storytelling. He relished that role in his put up-NBA career, with advert campaigns for Body Armor, a series of young person books, and his animated quick film pricey Basketball, which won an Oscar in 2018.

How Kobe Bryant is Inspiring the Next Generation

Kobe Bryant is one of the quality players in basketball history. A 5-time NBA champion, 2008 NBA most treasured participant, 18-time NBA All megastar, and -time Olympic gold medalist with team U.S.A. amongst other accomplishments, Bryant retired on the give up of the 2015–2016 NBA seasons after playing for 20 seasons with the l. A. Lakers.

Bryant becomes not the simplest one of the maximum gifted, fierce, and aggressive basketball players this planet has ever witnessed, but also an exceedingly cerebral, clever, and insightful player, a "student of the sport," as we basketball lovers like to name those type of characters. Bryant is still (and will stay)a true savant, a professional that digs beneath the surface of the numbers and the superficial factors of the game to advantage priceless insights into opponents, plays, and tiny information that move unnoticed for anybody else.

At the 2016 ESPYS Awards, when asked about his subsequent steps after retiring, Bryant made clear his intentions to commit himself to the adolescents in unique approaches.

"the largest key, I think, is inspiring the subsequent technology of athletes, and how to do this, and that I think content material is an incredibly effective tool of inspiring the next era of athletes, and that´s what I´m looking forward to doing."

After retiring, Bryant didn´t waste any time in venturing into his passion for uplifting the next technology. He kicked off his "retirement" life with the production and ebook of pricey Basketball, a love letter to the game of basketball in the layout of an animated brief. On this manufacturing, with the help of extraordinary minds like animator Glen Keane and composer John Williams, Bryant expresses his love for the sport, picturing himself as a child with dreams of turning into one of the greatest ever to play. The tone of the film, that's spectacularly animated, is noticeably inspirational and narrates Kobe´s route to turning into one of the maximum dominant players in records. Pricey Basketball became an instant achievement and gained the 2018 Academy Award for the great animated quick movie.

Believe enjoyment organization, the employer that produced the fast film furnished a great summary of its essence:

"Directed by using Academy-Award prevailing Disney animator, Glen Keane, and scored by using OSCAR® triumphing composer, John Williams, the hand-drawn movie speaks at once to the sport of basketball, and conveys Kobe's gratitude, love, and ardor for the game before leaving it at the back of."

A long way from feeling content material with triumphing an Oscar brief after retiring, Kobe endured cultivating his ardor to train kids lessons from his observations and attitude during his extremely good adventure as an expert NBA participant. These days, he launched The Wizard series, a 5-e-book collection written via author Wesley King, and providing a story with the aid of Kobe Bryant, geared in the direction of teens wherein "5 basketball teammates offer money owed of a ten-day training camp in this inspirational yet choppy myth.

While requested by way of Jimmy Fallon approximately his intentions with this e-book series, Bryant supplied a super photograph of his philosophy and what he thinks is critical to train those younger generations:

"The essential issue on this story is (that) it´s a tale of self-reputation. All of us have fears; we all have anxieties, things of that nature; however, we can forget about them. While you ignore them, they fester and feature manipulate over you, and what those younger men need to study through magic is a way to have the courage to face the one's fears and use the one's fears to help themselves be better basketball players and higher humans through it."

Kobe isn't doing any of this due to the fact there's an urgent want for brand new skills in the NBA. The game of basketball has in no way been in better shape. No matter the relatively latest retirements of iconic players from the 2000s, like Kobe Bryant, Kevin Garnett, Paul Pierce, Tim Duncan, and Manu Ginóbili, among others, the void left by way of these legends is already being stuffed way to the irruption and explosion of younger stars in their mid-20s like Giannis Antetokounmpo, Joel Embiid, Ben Simmons, or Nikola Jokic, and projected to maintain with growing stars of their early 20s like Devin Booker, Luka Doncic, or Trae young. The expertise pipeline is full of younger gamers that are making an impact at the NBA, collegiate, and international ranges. In different phrases, the NBA´s achievement and abundance of skills aren't going away any time soon.

No matter pronouncing he desires to encourage "the following era of athletes," Kobe isn't always directing his efforts just towards teaching what it takes to get to the best level. The chances of creating it to the NBA are extraordinarily slender, and Bryant´s mission is a lot broader than that. Together with his message, he is also showcasing the values of basketball as a larger-than-life detail, and inspiring the more youthful generations to embody the values of a group game that functions teamwork, sacrifice, and private and collective attempt as its principal traits.

No matter the actual quality and content material of The Wizenard series, it's far excellent information that a parent of Bryant´s stature and relevance is freeing a book collection, and emphasizing the benefits and the importance of studying alongside the method.

In an incredible article detailing Kobe´s new endeavors, SLAM mag´s Tzvi Twersky perfectly sums up Kobe´s aim together with his latest e-book series:

"the father of 4 women — and hero/villain to thousands of other people — wants his tomes to enlarge the YA style and to make studying greater accessible to younger athletes. He wishes it to learn in faculties nationally and to affect change globally:

`To me,´ says Bryant, `Wizenard is successful already. It's distinct from sports. In sports, the goal is to win a championship. With this stuff, if one person touches that ebook and is impacted deeply, then that's an achievement.´

Every other way in which Bryant is impacting the more youthful generations is education. Bryant is devoting himself to training his daughter and her crew with the principle purpose of permitting a number of them to play college basketball, striving to instill in them the identical paintings ethic that got him to be one of the excellent. He currently advised Jimmy Fallon:

We exercise each day. Three days per week isn't always going to get you there. You bought to without a doubt work. We run the triangle offense (a tremendously advanced system that Bryant used to play in when mythical educate Phil Jackson coached him).

Basketball, and lots of different regions of life, want humans like Kobe Bryant, who not handiest paintings extraordinarily tough to excel in what they do; however that also need to bypass down the torch to the subsequent era, to make contributions to kids´ schooling, and do everything viable to do so. For the girls, Kobe now coaches. It's far simply a deal with to have

Kobe Bryant as their coach, but it is also a privilege for the bigger public to pick out the brain of a legend, each on and rancid the basketball courtroom.

Printed in Great Britain
by Amazon